THE LIBRARY OF WHY?™

Why Do Some Animals Shed Their Skin?

Patricia J. Murphy

The Rosen Publishing Group's
PowerKids Press™
New York

To Bailey, with love

Published in 2004 by The Rosen Publishing Group, Inc.
29 East 21st Street, New York, NY 10010

First Edition

Editor: Frances E. Ruffin
Book Design: Danielle Primiceri
Layout: Michael de Guzman and Nick Sciacca

Photo Credits: Cover © Linda Lewis,Frank Lane Picture Agency/CORBIS; p. 4 © John R. MacGregor/Peter Arnold, Inc.; pp. 7 © S.J. Krasemann/Peter Arnold, Inc.; p. 8 © Zig Leszezynski/Animals Animals; p. 11 (top) © Digital Stock (bottom) © S.J. Krasemann/Peter Arnold, Inc.; p.12 © Juan Manuel Renjifo/Animals Animals; p. 15 © Jeffrey L. Rotman/Peter Arnold, Inc.; p. 16 © Donna Ikenberry/Animals Animals; p.19 © Jennie Woodcock; Reflections Photolibrary/CORBIS; p. 20 © Index Stock Imagery, Inc.

Murphy, Patricia J., 1963–
Why do some animals shed their skin? / by Patricia J. Murphy.— 1st ed.
     p. cm. — (The library of why)
Summary: Explains what molting is and what causes it, then looks at how snakes, insects, crabs, birds, dogs, and cats shed skin, skeletons, or fur.
ISBN 0-8239-6237-7 (lib. bdg.)
1. Animals—Juvenile literature. 2. Molting—Juvenile literature. [1. Animals. 2. Molting.] I. Title. II. The library of why?
QL49 .M88 2003
573.5—dc21

2001005467

Manufactured in the United States of America

Contents

Why Do Animals Lose Their Coverings?

Like the cover of a book or the wrapping paper on a birthday gift, every animal has a skin or an outer covering. Humans and snakes have skin. Most **mammals** have fur. Birds have feathers. Insects and crabs have outside skeletons, or **exoskeletons**. These outside coverings protect the soft **organs** inside our bodies. They also act as shields to help keep germs, dust, and dirt from entering the body. Many animals, such as snakes, water birds, and insects, lose, or **molt**, all of their body coverings at once.

This brown snake has just shed its skin. Humans and most birds shed their coverings a little at a time.

5

What Causes Molting?

An animal sheds or molts its outer covering as a way of **adapting** to its **environment**. When snakes outgrow their old skins, they shed them. For some animals, changes in daylight or changes in the season set off a chemical in their brains. Scientists believe that this chemical causes an animal to molt. An animal that has an exoskeleton, such as an insect or a **crustacean**, makes a molting liquid that helps the new covering to grow. It also helps the old covering break away from the animal's body. The new covering then dries and hardens.

Some animals, like elk and deer, molt their horns or antlers in the winter and regrow them in the spring. ▶

Why Do Snakes Shed Their Skin?

A snake's skin is made up of many small scales that are made of **keratin.** These scales are arranged like tiles on a bathroom floor. A snake's scales get a lot of wear. A snake replaces worn scales with new ones by shedding its skin. It must also shed to grow. When a snake sheds its skin, its eyes become covered with a cloudy liquid. The snake does not eat during this time. It cannot see. It spends much of its time hiding in a damp place. To help peel off its old skin, the snake rubs its jaw on rocks, tree bark, or the ground.

◀ *This corn snake is in the process of shedding its skin. Young snakes shed their skins many times as they grow.*

9

Why Do Other Animals Molt?

Mammals, like deer and wolves, grow heavy winter coats before the first snowfall. These new winter coats trap their body heat to keep them warm in winter. They molt these coats in the spring, when the weather becomes warmer. Some mammals, like the **Arctic** fox and the snowshoe rabbit, molt in the fall to replace their dark-colored fur with thicker, white fur to keep them warm. Their white fur helps them to adapt to a snowy environment. By blending into the snow, they can catch **prey** or can avoid **predators**.

The Arctic fox, at the top, and the snowshoe rabbit, at the bottom, are wearing their white winter coats. ▶

Arctic Fox ▶

◀ **Snowshoe Rabbit**

How Do Insects Shed Their Skeletons?

An insect starts molting by breaking down its tough outer shell, known as its exoskeleton. This outside skeleton is made from chitin, a material that is like our fingernails. The outer skeleton becomes part of the new exoskeleton growing below it. Once the new exoskeleton is ready, the insect splits open its old body covering and wiggles out. The insect pumps air or water into its body. This allows the insect to make its body fit before its new exoskeleton hardens. Insects will molt many times before they become adults.

◀ *This grasshopper is molting its exoskeleton. Once they become adults, insects never molt again.*

How Do Crabs Molt?

As do insects, crabs and other crustaceans have outside coverings that are their skeletons. When the crab's covering becomes too small for its growing body, it molts and builds a new exoskeleton under its old one. Soon the crab finds a dark place to molt. There it fills its old exoskeleton with water. This allows the crab to crack it open and to discard its old exoskeleton. Before the new exoskeleton hardens, the crab stretches its body like an old sweater. This helps it to fit its larger body into the new exoskeleton.

Crabs, like this one, molt many times in their lives. If a crab loses one of its legs, it can grow a new one when it molts. ▶

Why Do Birds Lose Their Feathers?

Many birds molt all of their feathers in late summer or early fall. When birds' feathers become worn or broken, the birds may molt only a few feathers at a time to replace them. When a bird molts, its new feathers push out the old ones. Birds living in cold climates molt and grow thick, downy feathers before winter to keep them warm. Birds often grow brightly colored feathers to attract mates. Regrowing dull feathers helps to prevent birds from becoming prey.

Some water birds, like this king penguin, molt all of their feathers at once. Baby birds must molt a few times to look like adults.

Why Do Dogs and Cats Shed Their Fur?

Fur is made of different kinds of hair. Fur helps to keep animals warm in cold weather, and it helps to keep them cool in hot weather. When cats and dogs shed their fur, they are molting. As do most mammals, dogs and cats molt their fur coats twice each year. They may grow thicker fur coats in the winter, and shed those fur coats for the warmer weather. It may seem that they molt year-round. If you have a cat or a dog, you can see its fur left behind on your clothing, your sofa, and on your other items.

When mammals molt, we call it shedding. Shedding fur is another way that some animals molt. ▶

Do Humans Molt?

Yes, humans molt. During a cold, dry winter day, if we rub the skin from our arms or from the backs of our hands on a dark-colored piece of clothing, we can see dried skin **cells**. The human skin is made of tiny skin cells. Each year we shed thousands of dead skin cells, and we regrow thousands of new cells. We also lose and replace the hair on our heads and our bodies. When humans fail to regrow some or all of their hair, it's called baldness.

◀ *The skin is the human body's largest organ.*

How Do Animals Care for Their Skin?

Whether body coverings are made of skin, fur, feathers, scales, or exoskeletons, they protect people and animals from the outside world. Some animals do special jobs to take care of their "skins." Snakes and other reptiles choose humid, or wet, places to live. To help them fly, birds preen to make their feathers lie straight. It is important that people should remember to use sunscreen when going in the sun. This can help prevent sunburn and possibly skin cancer, because we're not like snakes. We can't shed our skins all at once.

Glossary

adapting (uh-DAPT-ing) When an animal changes to fit into its environment.

Arctic (ARK-tik) Referring to the northernmost regions on Earth.

cells (SELZ) Many tiny units that make up all living things.

crustacean (krus-TAY-shun) An animal that is an invertebrate with a hard shell, limbs, and antennae, for example, a crab.

environment (en-VY-urn-ment) All the living things and the conditions that make up a place.

exoskeletons (ek-soh-SKEH-leh-tinz) The hard outer shells of insects or crustaceans.

keratin (KER-uh-tun) A material that is found in human hair and nails and in animal fur, scales, and horns.

mammals (MA-mulz) Warm-blooded animals that have backbones, hair or fur, and that feed milk to their young.

molt (MOHLT) When an animal sheds its skin, fur, or other outer covering.

organs (OR-genz) Parts of an animal or a plant that do a specific thing.

predators (PREH-duh-terz) Animals that kill other animals for food.

prey (PRAY) An animal that is hunted and eaten by another animal.

Index

Web Sites

Due to the changing nature of Internet links, PowerKids Press has developed an online list of Web sites related to the subject of this book. This site is updated regularly. Please use this link to access the list:

www.powerkidslinks.com/low/animshed/